THE MAGNIFICENT BOOK OF DINOSAURS

AND OTHER PREHISTORIC CREATURES

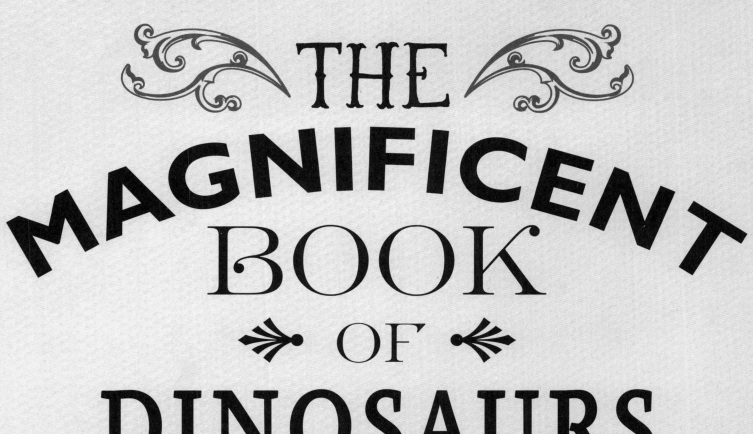

THE MAGNIFICENT BOOK OF DINOSAURS

AND OTHER PREHISTORIC CREATURES

ILLUSTRATED BY
Rudolf Farkas

WRITTEN BY
Tom Jackson

Silver Dolphin

Silver Dolphin Books
An imprint of Printers Row Publishing Group
A division of Readerlink Distribution Services, LLC
10350 Barnes Canyon Road, Suite 100, San Diego, CA 92121
www.silverdolphinbooks.com

All notations of errors or omissions should be addressed to Silver Dolphin Books, Editorial Department, at the
above address. All other correspondence (author inquiries, permissions) concerning the content of this book
should be addressed to:
Weldon Owen
King's Road Publishing
The Plaza
535 King's Road
London SW10 0SZ, UK
www.weldonowen.co.uk
www.bonnierpublishing.com

Library of Congress Cataloging-in-Publication Data

Names: Jackson, Tom, 1972- | Farkas, Rudolf, illustrator.
Title: The magnificent book of dinosaurs and other prehsitoric creatures / illustrated by Rudolf Farkas; written by Tom Jackson.
Description: San Diego, CA : Silver Dolphin Books, 2017. | Audience: Age 8.
Identifiers: LCCN 2016021389 | ISBN 9781626867437
Subjects: LCSH: Dinosaurs--Juvenile literature. | Paleontology--Mesozoic--Juvenile literature.
Classification: LCC QE861.5 .J3345 2017 | DDC 567.9--dc23
LC record available at https://lccn.loc.gov/2016021389

Manufactured, printed, and assembled in Shenzhen, China.
Second printing, October 2017. RRD/10/17
21 20 19 18 17 2 3 4 5 6

Introduction

Millions of years ago, during the Mesozoic era, prehistoric reptiles called dinosaurs roamed the Earth. It was a much different Earth then. The continents were connected, the land that people live on today was covered in water, and lush forests provided the perfect environment for dinosaurs to thrive. But about 65 million years ago, a large asteroid struck Earth and caused the dinosaurs to become extinct. So everything we know about them comes from the bits and pieces of their bodies that became fossils.

This book features stunning illustrations of the mysterious dinosaurs that once lived on Earth—from gigantic plant-eaters to swift and deadly predators. Each page showcases a different creature, such as Tyrannosaurus rex or Stegosaurus, with fascinating facts that illustrate how the dinosaurs lived.

Which dinosaur had thick thumb spikes? Which one had a tail like a club that it used to whack enemies? Which dinosaur was twice as tall as a giraffe? Discover all of these answers and more as you enter *The Magnificent Book of Dinosaurs and Other Prehistoric Creatures.*

Fact file

Found in: North America

Meaning of name: Three-horned face

Length: 30 feet

Weight: 12,000 pounds

Lived: 67–65 million years ago

Diet: Plants

Contents

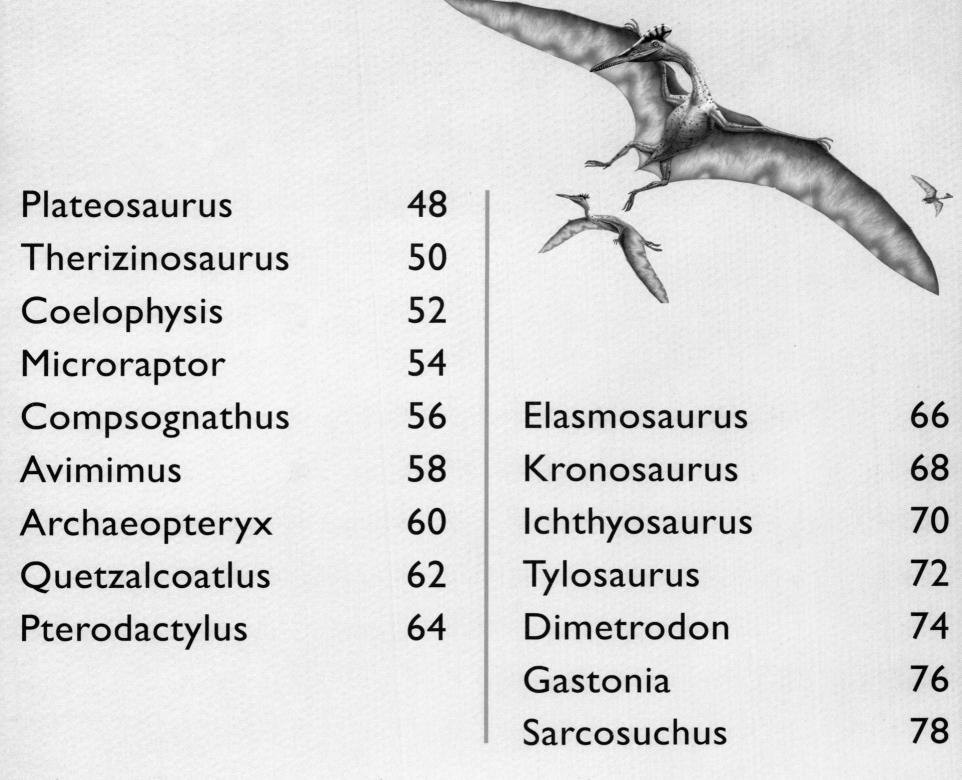

Tyrannosaurus rex

T. rex's curved teeth could grow up to 12 inches long.

Research suggests that T. rex could swallow up to 500 pounds of meat in one gulp.

This dinosaur's small arms had long, hooked claws for ripping up meat and for hanging on to its prey.

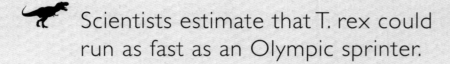 Scientists estimate that T. rex could run as fast as an Olympic sprinter.

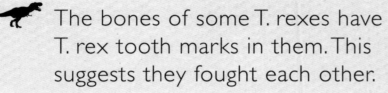 The bones of some T. rexes have T. rex tooth marks in them. This suggests they fought each other.

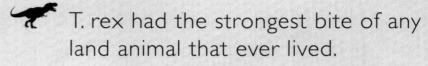 T. rex had the strongest bite of any land animal that ever lived.

In addition to hunting for food, T. rex also ate the remains of dead dinosaurs.

Fact file

Found in: North America

Meaning of name: King of the tyrant lizards

Length: 40 feet

Weight: 15,400 pounds

Lived: 67–65 million years ago

Diet: Other dinosaurs

Giganotosaurus

This giant hunter was even larger than T. rex, but it was more slender and a faster runner.

Evidence suggests that Giganotosaurus teamed up into hunting packs to attack herds of plant-eating dinosaurs.

Its long, thin tail helped the massive animal stay balanced as it ran.

Giganotosaurus's head was more than five feet long!

Giganotosaurus is the largest land predator that has ever been found.

Each of its teeth had sawlike edges, which allowed it to cut through flesh easily.

Fact file

Found in: Argentina

Meaning of name: Giant southern lizard

Length: 43 feet

Weight: 28,000 pounds

Lived: 99–97 million years ago

Diet: Other dinosaurs

Allosaurus

Allosaurus had hooked teeth, which would have helped it to hold on to its struggling prey.

Allosaurus sometimes lost teeth during fights, but they grew back throughout its life.

This hunter may have killed its prey by biting their necks.

The dinosaur had tough ridges on its forehead, which protected its eyes during fights.

A powerful sense of smell helped Allosaurus to find prey.

Fact file

Found in: North America, Europe

Meaning of name: Different lizard

Length: 39 feet

Weight: 4,400 pounds

Lived: 155–150 million years ago

Diet: Other dinosaurs

 Allosaurus was one of the most common predators in North America during the late Jurassic period.

 This dinosaur is known to have preyed on stegosaurs.

13

Deinonychus

Fact file

Found in: North America

Meaning of name: Terrible claw

Length: 10 feet

Weight: 165 pounds

Lived: 120–110 million years ago

Diet: Other dinosaurs

This fast-running dinosaur could kill its prey by slashing them with the long, curved claw on each hind limb.

The large killer claws were retractable, so they did not scrape along the ground—this kept the claws sharp.

Scientists think Deinonychus may have used its hooked claws to climb trees to escape from larger hunters.

Deinonychus was probably covered in feathers that were similar to those of today's birds, but they did not help it to fly.

Deinonychus ran along on two legs. Its front legs were used for grabbing prey.

Deinonychus had a relatively large brain for its body size, so it was probably one of the smarter dinosaurs.

Utahraptor

- The long bones of a Utahraptor were hollow but strong. The bones did not weigh very much, which may have helped Utahraptor move quickly.

- This tall hunter could smell its prey from about a mile away.

- A coat of feathers probably kept it warm and helped it to attract mates.

- Utahraptor may have flapped its arms like wings in order to help it climb steep slopes.

Utahraptor probably had good eyesight, so it could spot prey from far away.

Scientists think that Utahraptor could jump 15 feet in one leap.

Evidence suggests that Utahraptor may have hunted in packs to kill larger animals.

Fact file

Found in: North America

Meaning of name: Utah's predator

Length: 23 feet

Weight: 1,100 pounds

Lived: 125 million years ago

Diet: Other dinosaurs

Spinosaurus

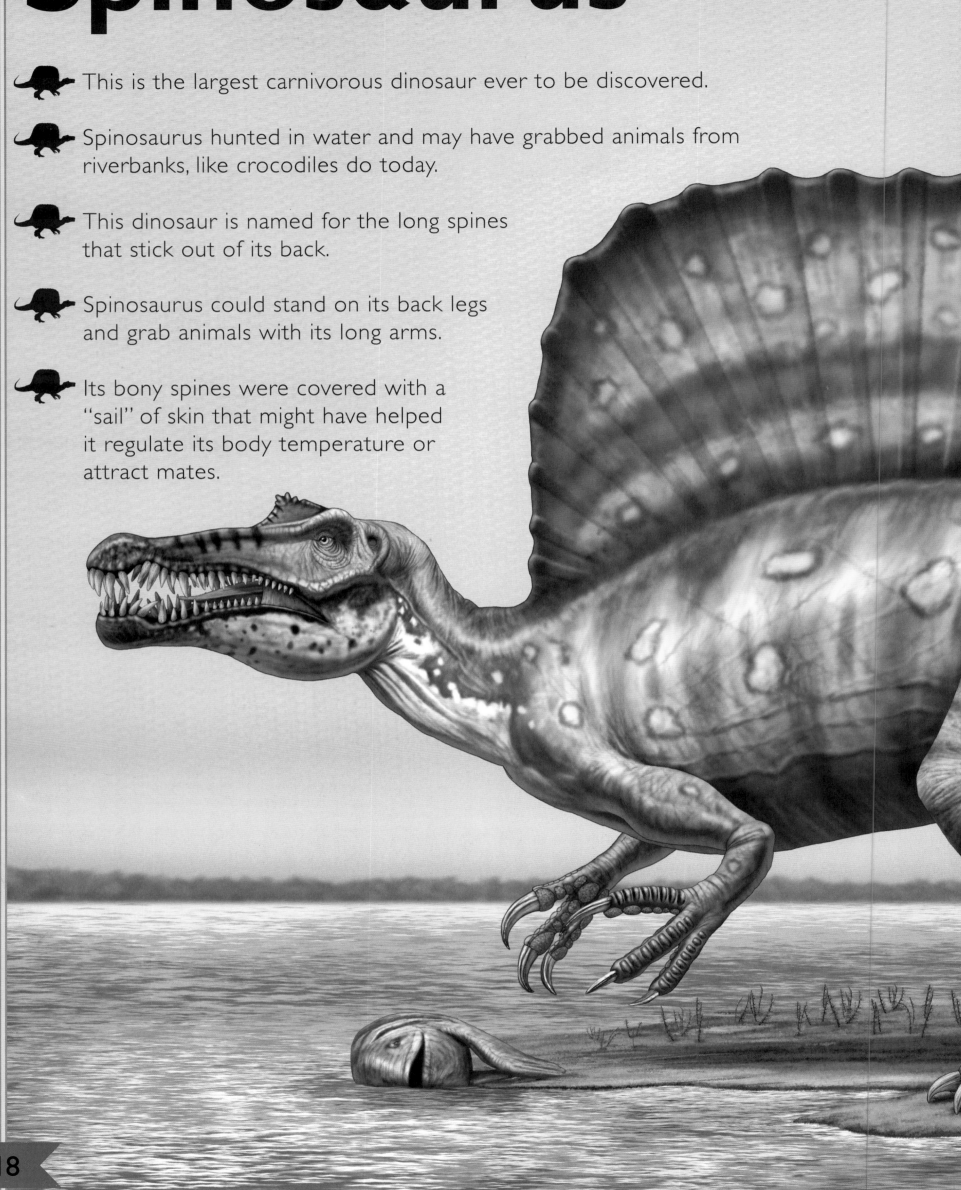

- This is the largest carnivorous dinosaur ever to be discovered.

- Spinosaurus hunted in water and may have grabbed animals from riverbanks, like crocodiles do today.

- This dinosaur is named for the long spines that stick out of its back.

- Spinosaurus could stand on its back legs and grab animals with its long arms.

- Its bony spines were covered with a "sail" of skin that might have helped it regulate its body temperature or attract mates.

Spinosaurus had nostrils on the top of its snout, so it could hide below the water with just the top of its head showing.

This hunter had sensors on its snout that helped it detect water currents and weak electrical signals made by prey swimming nearby.

Fact file

Found in: North Africa

Meaning of name: Spine lizard

Length: 46 feet

Weight: 6,000 pounds

Lived: 112–97 million years ago

Diet: Fish

19

Iguanodon

This dinosaur's fossils were discovered in 1820. It was the second type of dinosaur to be identified by scientists.

Iguanodon had a thick spiked claw on each thumb.

Early scientists mistakenly thought Iguanodon's thumb spike was a nose horn.

Found in: Europe, North America, Asia, Africa

Meaning of name: Iguana tooth

Length: 35 feet

Weight: 12,000 pounds

Lived: 140–110 million years ago

Diet: Plants

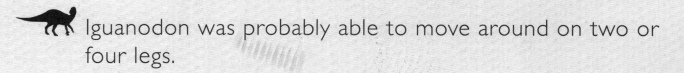 Iguanodon was probably able to move around on two or four legs.

 Iguanodon may have used its thumb spike to rip off leaves and twigs from branches.

Evidence suggests that these plant-eaters lived in large herds.

Iguanodon could use its clawed thumb to defend itself from other dinosaurs.

Triceratops

Triceratops used its long horns to fight off attacks by large meat-eaters like T. rex.

The back of Triceratops's head was covered with a large bony frill that protected its neck from predators.

Triceratops had the biggest skull of any land animal that has ever lived. One fossilized skull measured more than eight feet long.

🦖 The horns above its eyes were more than three feet long.

🦖 Triceratops had a hooked beak that could cut up leaves.

🦖 Triceratops was not a fast runner, but it likely charged into its enemies to chase them away.

Stygimoloch

- This dinosaur had a domed skull covered in sharp, pointed horns.

- Scientists believe that the creature's spiked head was used mostly for display, but it might have been used in fights as well.

- Rival Stygimoloch probably did not butt each other with their heads, but pushed against each other's sides instead.

- Stygimoloch had small, triangular teeth for chewing tough leaves.

Fact file

Found in: North America

Meaning of name: Demon of the river Styx

Length: 10 feet

Weight: 170 pounds

Lived: 67–65 million years ago

Diet: Plants

As the dinosaur got older, its skull became rounder and grew more spikes.

Stygimoloch was a pachycephalosaur, which means "thick-headed lizard."

Evidence suggests that Stygimoloch lived in herds.

Psittacosaurus

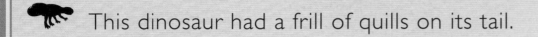

This dinosaur had a frill of quills on its tail.

It had a bony beak for chopping off the tops of shrubs.

Psittacosaurus was a fast runner and could run on two legs while using its tail for balance.

Psittacosaurus spent most of its time upright on its back legs, and may have used its forelimbs to grasp objects.

Fact file

Found in: Asia

Meaning of name: Parrot lizard

Length: 6.5 feet

Weight: 110 pounds

Lived: 120–100 million years ago

Diet: Plants

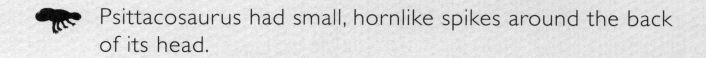 Psittacosaurus had small, hornlike spikes around the back of its head.

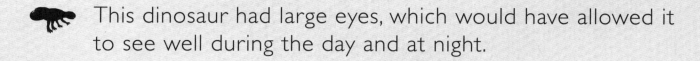 This dinosaur had large eyes, which would have allowed it to see well during the day and at night.

Some scientists have suggested that Psittacosaurus could swim by using its frilly tail as a paddle.

Stegosaurus

Fact file

Found in: North America, Europe

Meaning of name: Roof lizard

Length: 30 feet

Weight: 6,000 pounds

Lived: 155–150 million years ago

Diet: Plants

 This dinosaur's brain was about the size of a small apple.

 Stegosaurus could use its spiked tail to defend itself from predators.

 The plates along Stegosaurus's spine may have offered some protection against attackers.

 Scientists believe the plates also absorbed sunlight and helped Stegosaurus control its body temperature.

 At first, scientists thought the plates stuck out sideways, making a "roof," which is how it got its name. (In Greek, stegos means "roof.")

 Stegosaurus could not chew its food, and instead swallowed it in large chunks.

 Stegosaurus could not lift its head very high, so it grazed on small ferns that grew low to the ground.

Ankylosaurus

- This dinosaur's back was protected by thick, bony plates and spikes.

- Some ankylosaurs had a large bony club at the end of their tails.

- The tail club was used to hit attackers.

A whack from the tail club was strong enough to break a T. rex's leg!

Even the eyelids of Ankylosaurus had small bony plates for extra protection.

Ankylosaurus was very wide and had short legs. This made it difficult to knock over in fights.

Ankylosaurus lived in mountainous regions and ate all kinds of plants.

Fact file

Found in: North America

Meaning of name: Fused lizard

Length: 35 feet

Weight: 8,000 pounds

Lived: 74–67 million years ago

Diet: Plants

Velociraptor

Velociraptor is one of the most famous dinosaurs. It was much smaller than many people think, only about the size of a large turkey—although it was probably more fierce.

Velociraptor had long arms with hooked claws for reaching forward and grabbing prey.

This hunter used its claws and teeth to attack prey.

Velociraptor was covered with small feathers, which could have been used to attract a mate or to keep its body warm.

Fact file

Found in: Mongolia

Meaning of name: Swift seizer (aka, speedy thief)

Length: 6 feet

Weight: 33 pounds

Lived: 85–70 million years ago

Diet: Small mammals, birds, and small dinosaurs

Velociraptor had a large brain relative to its body size, which suggests it was one of the more intelligent dinosaur species.

Velociraptor could run at speeds up to 40 mph for short distances, so it could catch prey easily.

Brachiosaurus

 Brachiosaurus was twice as tall as a modern giraffe.

 This massive dinosaur stripped pine needles and leaves from the tops of tall trees.

 Brachiosaurus had large openings at the top of its head. They may have been used to make loud calls.

 Brachiosaurus's neck usually pointed upward—it could lower its head to the ground, but this was rare.

Fact file

Found in: North America
Meaning of name: Arm lizard
Length: 85 feet
Weight: 150,000 pounds
Lived: 155–140 million years ago
Diet: Plants

Brachiosaurus's rear legs were more than six feet long.

It ate about 400 to 600 pounds of food every day.

The dinosaur had just 12 large bones in its long neck.

Diplodocus

- Diplodocus was the longest land animal to ever live on Earth.

- The tail of a Diplodocus made up about half of this dinosaur's body length.

- Scientists believe that Diplodocus used its long, pointed tail as a whip to fight off attackers.

- Diplodocus's tail contained 80 bones, far more than any other dinosaur.

- Scientists believe that Diplodocus had air sacs deep inside its body that helped to pump air through its lungs.

Fact file

Found in: North America

Meaning of name: Double beam

Length: 110 feet

Weight: 33,000 pounds

Lived: 155–145 million years ago

Diet: Plants

Diplodocus's back legs were longer than its front ones, which shows it lowered its head to feed on plants close to the ground.

Diplodocus could not chew its food. Instead, it swallowed stones to help grind up food in its stomach.

Dreadnoughtus

- Dreadnoughtus is the largest dinosaur ever discovered.

- Dreadnoughtus weighed 84,000 pounds—that is about as much as eight African elephants.

- A dinosaur this big had very few enemies.

- Dreadnoughtus is a recent discovery. Only two fossils have been found, and both were dug up in 2005.

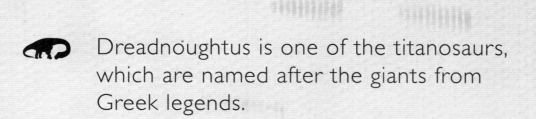 Dreadnoughtus is one of the titanosaurs, which are named after the giants from Greek legends.

Scientists wonder if the fossils of this giant dinosaur found so far are from young animals. If so, Dreadnoughtus may have been even larger than we know!

Fact file

Found in: South America
Meaning of name: Fear nothing
Length: 85 feet
Weight: 84,000 pounds
Lived: 84–66 million years ago
Diet: Plants

Oviraptor

- The first fossil of this dinosaur was found lying beside a nest full of eggs.

- Experts first thought that this dinosaur was raiding the nest and named the creature Oviraptor, or "egg thief." However, we now know she was a mother guarding her own eggs.

- Oviraptor probably had a brightly colored feathered tail that fanned out like a peacock's.

- Oviraptor had a crest on its head. This might have been used as a weapon, or it could have been another way of showing off.

- Oviraptor had large eyes for spotting danger—if it saw a hunter, it could run away quickly.

- This dinosaur was related to Velociraptor and other hunters, but it probably ate both plants and small animals.

- Oviraptor had no teeth, but it had bone spikes inside its mouth that may have been used for cracking open shellfish.

Fact file

Found in: Mongolia

Meaning of name: Egg thief

Length: 6.5 feet

Weight: 55 pounds

Lived: 85–75 million years ago

Diet: Plants, small animals, and shellfish

Maiasaura

- Maiasaura lived in large herds of more than a thousand animals.

- The female Maiasaura laid their eggs at the same time, creating a huge nesting colony.

- Each female Maiasaura made a nest mound in the ground to hold her eggs.

- The Maiasaura mother laid her eggs in a spiral or circle shape within the nest mound.

- After the eggs hatched, the babies stayed on the mound and were fed by their mother.

Fact file

Found in: North America

Meaning of name: Mother lizard

Length: 30 feet

Weight: 8,000 pounds

Lived: 80–75 million years ago

Diet: Plants

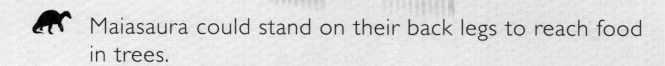 Maiasaura could stand on their back legs to reach food in trees.

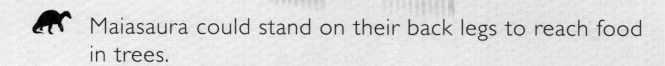 Herds of Maiasaura probably returned to the same nesting sites each year.

Corythosaurus

- Corythosaurus was one of the hadrosaurid, or duck-billed, dinosaurs, which are named for their wide, flat mouths.

- This dinosaur had a bone crest on its head. Scientists think this might have become brightly colored during the breeding season.

- The duck-bill mouth was used to crush the needles, twigs, and cones that grew on pine trees.

- The crest was hollow and made Corythosaurus's calls louder.

Fact file

Found in: North America

Meaning of name: Helmet lizard

Length: 33 feet

Weight: 8,000 pounds

Lived: 80–65 million years ago

Diet: Plants

Corythosaurus lived in forests and waded through swamps.

Corythosaurus likely had a more sensitive sense of hearing than most dinosaurs—even though its ears were hidden inside its skull.

The large eyes of Corythosaurus tell us that this animal could see well during the day and at night.

Parasaurolophus

- Parasaurolophus had a long, tube-shaped horn on its head.

- The horn was hollow, with air passages running from the top of the dinosaur's head to its nostrils.

- The passages may have been used like a trumpet to produce a loud honking noise.

- Parasaurolophus walked on four legs but could run on its back legs to flee danger.

- Scientists believe that older Parasaurolophus males with the longest horns were the herd leaders.

Fact file

Found in: North America

Meaning of name: Near crested lizard

Length: 30 feet

Weight: 7,000 pounds

Lived: 76–66 million years ago

Diet: Pine needles and leaves

The air tubes in the crest may have also helped Parasaurolophus control its body temperature.

 Evidence suggests that Parasaurolophus herds migrated higher up mountains for the summer and came down again in the winter.

Plateosaurus

- This was a very early type of dinosaur. It lived 150 million years before T. rex.

- Plateosaurus was an early relative of the giant plant-eating dinosaurs, like Diplodocus and Brachiosaurus.

- Plateosaurus walked on two legs and used its clawed hands to pull branches to its mouth.

- Its thick tail worked like a third leg to keep it balanced as it reached up into tall trees.

- This dinosaur had small, pointed teeth that shredded its leafy food.

- Plateosaurus had a big hooked claw on its thumb, which might have been used in fights.

Fact file

Found in: Europe

Meaning of name: Broad lizard

Length: 26 feet

Weight: 6,000 pounds

Lived: 210 million years ago

Diet: Plants

Therizinosaurus

This dinosaur is named for the giant claws on its hands, which look like curved knives, or scythes. (In Greek, *therizo* means "to cut or mow.")

Therizinosaurus had three claws on each hand, which could grow to be more than three feet long.

Evidence suggests that this dinosaur was probably covered in feathers like its relatives Velociraptor and Deinonychus.

Therizinosaurus likely had flat teeth and a beak, suggesting that it was not a hunter; it would have eaten plants and perhaps insects.

Fact file

Found in: Mongolia

Meaning of name: Scythe lizard

Length: 33 feet

Weight: 11,000 pounds

Lived: 85–70 million years ago

Diet: Plants and insects

Scientists believe that Therizinosaurus's claws were probably used to reach leafy branches.

Therizinosaurus may also have used its claws for digging up roots or termite mounds.

Therizinosaurus was very tall and could fight off most enemies with its slashing claws.

Coelophysis

- A slender hunter, Coelophysis was one of the first dinosaurs to evolve.

- This fast-running dinosaur preyed on small animals.

- Large herds of Coelophysis gathered at watering holes to drink or eat fish.

- This dinosaur was named for its hollow bones. (In Greek, *coelos* means "hollow," and *physis* means "form.") Today, though, we know that most dinosaur bones were hollow.

Fact file

Found in: North America

Meaning of name: Hollow form

Length: 10 feet

Weight: 40 pounds

Lived: 205–195 million years ago

Diet: Fish and small reptiles

More than 1,000 Coelophysis fossils were found in one location in New Mexico.

Coelophysis was not a strong dinosaur, but it probably hunted in packs to take down larger prey.

Microraptor

- This small feathered dinosaur had four wings—two on its arms and two on its legs.

- Microraptor had claws on its wings, which it used for climbing trees.

- This dinosaur used its four wings to glide between trees to escape danger.

- Scientists believe that Microraptor could not take off from the ground.

- Microraptor could have used its gliding wings to pounce on lizards living in trees.

- This dinosaur probably also scooped up fish while gliding over water.

- Microraptor was likely a nighttime hunter; fossils suggest that its eyes provided excellent vision in the dark.

- Microraptor is the smallest known dinosaur species.

Fact file

Found in: China
Meaning of name: Tiny seizer
Length: 2 feet
Weight: 2 pounds
Lived: 125–122 million years ago
Diet: Insects

Compsognathus

- This dinosaur was about the size of a large turkey.

- Scientists believe that Compsognathus chased its lizard prey through the undergrowth.

- Compsognathus hunted by sight using its large eyes, and could move quickly to capture prey.

- No other dinosaur fossils have been found near Compsognathus fossils, which suggests that it was the top predator in its habitat.

Fact file

Found in: Europe

Meaning of name: Elegant jaw

Length: 4 feet

Weight: 8 pounds

Lived: 150–140 million years ago

Diet: Insects and lizards

Compsognathus lived on islands in a sea that once covered eastern Europe and the Middle East.

Complete remains of lizards have been found inside Compsognathus fossils, which means that this dinosaur swallowed its prey whole.

Avimimus

- This dinosaur lived in what is now Mongolia, around 75 million years ago.

- Most of the bones in Avimimus's small arms were fused together like in a bird's wing.

- Avimimus could not fly, but it probably used its feathers to keep warm, or for display.

- Avimimus had a beak with small teeth, which meant it could eat both plants and animals.

Fact file

Found in: Asia

Meaning of name: Bird mimic

Length: 5 feet

Weight: 33 pounds

Lived: 80–75 million years ago

Diet: Plants, insects, and small lizards

Avimimus lived in an area that was covered by sand dunes; it used its speed to chase prey and to escape from predators.

Scientists believe that this dinosaur lived in flocks for safety.

Archaeopteryx

- Many scientists think that Archaeopteryx was not a dinosaur, but that it was one of the first birds.

- Archaeopteryx had a long, bony tail and sharp teeth.

- Scientists don't know if Archaeopteryx could fly from the ground—it probably glided out of trees instead.

- Archaeopteryx did not have big flying muscles like today's birds, so it could not stay in the air for long.

Fact file

Found in: Europe

Meaning of name: Ancient feather

Length: 1.5 feet

Weight: 2 pounds

Lived: 150 million years ago

Diet: Insects and lizards

This animal's small eyes suggest that it hunted during the day.

Scientists think that Archaeopteryx used its wings to help it stay up while it ran over the surface of a lake to hunt fish.

Evidence suggests Archaeopteryx would have grabbed prey with its mouth and held it there with its claws.

Quetzalcoatlus

- Quetzalcoatlus was one of the largest flying animals ever to have lived.

- Its wingspan was about the size of a small airplane.

- Quetzalcoatlus was not a dinosaur. It was an ancient flying reptile called a pterosaur.

- Scientists believe that this giant flier most likely fed on prey on the ground, like a stork or a crane.

- Quetzalcoatlus could walk on all fours with its wings folded out of the way.

Fact file

Found in: North America

Meaning of name: Feathered serpent god

Length: 35 feet (wingspan)

Weight: 500 pounds

Lived: 70–65 million years ago

Diet: Small dinosaurs, lizards, and mammals

Quetzalcoatlus could glide through the air for long periods at a time looking for food.

This creature is named after Quetzalcoatl, a feathered god worshipped by the Aztecs, who lived in what is now Mexico.

Pterodactylus

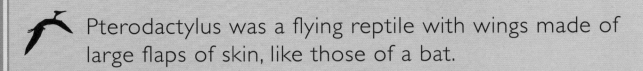 Pterodactylus was a flying reptile with wings made of large flaps of skin, like those of a bat.

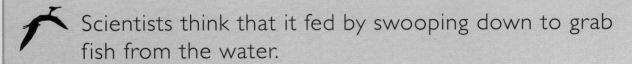 Scientists think that it fed by swooping down to grab fish from the water.

This creature was discovered in 1784, before dinosaurs were identified. It was the first flying reptile ever known.

The front of its wing was made from an extremely long, thin finger bone.

Pterodactylus, like other prehistoric flying reptiles, was not a dinosaur. These creatures belonged to a group of reptiles known as pterosaurs.

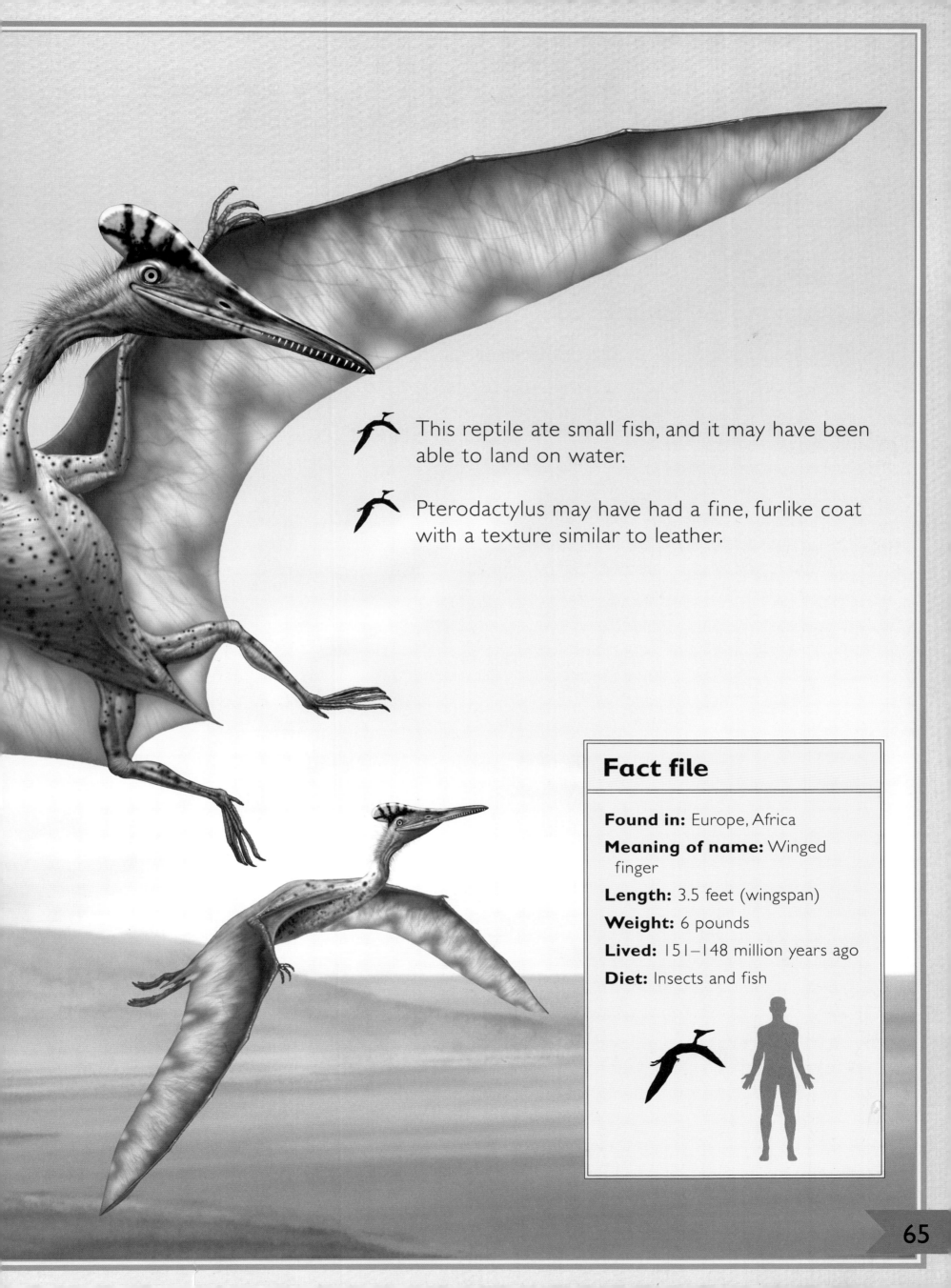

This reptile ate small fish, and it may have been able to land on water.

Pterodactylus may have had a fine, furlike coat with a texture similar to leather.

Fact file

Found in: Europe, Africa

Meaning of name: Winged finger

Length: 3.5 feet (wingspan)

Weight: 6 pounds

Lived: 151–148 million years ago

Diet: Insects and fish

Elasmosaurus

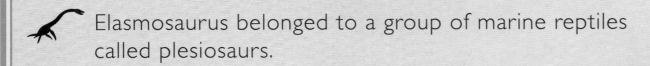

- Elasmosaurus belonged to a group of marine reptiles called plesiosaurs.

- It had a long, flexible neck that contained 71 bones.

- Its tail was much shorter—that had just 18 bones.

- Elasmosaurus lived in shallow seas and preyed on fish and squid.

- Evidence suggests that Elasmosaurus attacked fish from below, lunging upward with its long neck to catch them.

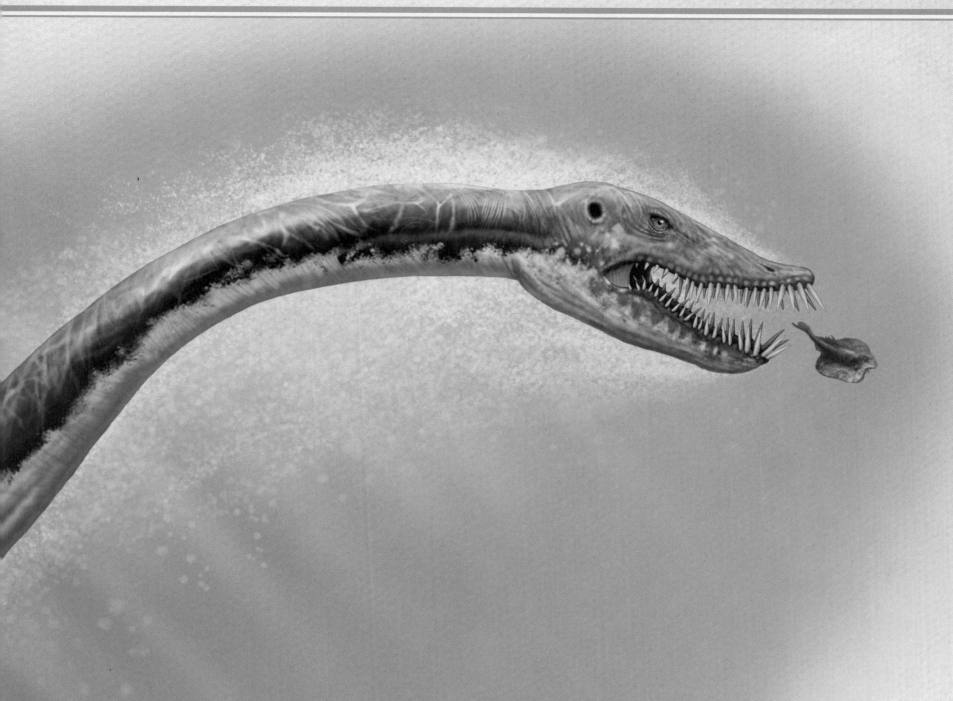

 This sea creature had flippers instead of legs, and could not walk on land.

 Scientists believe that Elasmosaurus did not lay eggs but gave birth to live babies in the water, like other plesiosaurs living at the same time.

Fact file

Found in: Shallow seas, especially in North America

Meaning of name: Thin plate lizard

Length: 45 feet

Weight: 6,000 pounds

Lived: 80 million years ago

Diet: Fish, squid, and shellfish

Kronosaurus

- This marine reptile had a huge jaw, which it used to crush the shells of its prey.

- It is a pliosaur, which were the largest and toughest hunters in the ancient seas.

Fact file

Found in: Shallow seas, worldwide

Meaning of name: Kronos's lizard

Length: 30 feet

Weight: 24,000 pounds

Lived: 110 million years ago

Diet: Fish, squid, and reptiles

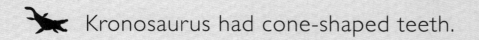 Kronosaurus had cone-shaped teeth.

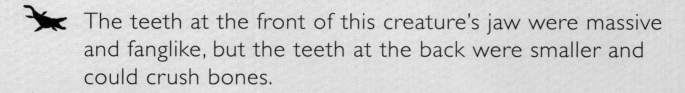 The teeth at the front of this creature's jaw were massive and fanglike, but the teeth at the back were smaller and could crush bones.

The reptile swam using four powerful flippers. It may also have been able to use its flippers to walk on land, like seals do today.

Kronosaurus probably fed like some modern crocodiles do, by twisting off large chunks of meat from its prey.

Kronosaurus had air-filled smell detectors on its snout that could be used to sniff out prey in the water.

Ichthyosaurus

- Ichthyosaurus was not a dinosaur but a marine reptile.

- It had huge eyes for seeing clearly in deep, dark water.

- Ichthyosaurus had sensitive ears hidden inside its head, which it may have used to detect prey by sensing their movement in the water.

- Ichthyosaurus breathed air, but it could not walk on land.

- This reptile gave birth to live babies in warm, shallow water.

Fact file

Found in: Oceans, worldwide

Meaning of name: Fish lizard

Length: 6 feet

Weight: 200 pounds

Lived: 200–190 million years ago

Diet: Fish and squid

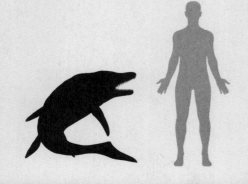

Ichthyosaurus looked a lot like a modern dolphin—but it was a reptile, not a mammal like the dolphin.

Ichthyosaurus mostly ate squid and some fish.

Tylosaurus

- This is one of the largest marine reptiles ever found.

- It is more closely related to today's monitor lizards than to dinosaurs or other ancient reptiles.

- Evidence suggests that this massive hunter attacked prey by ramming into it at full speed.

- Tylosaurus used its flippers for steering but was powered through the water by its long, flat tail.

- Tylosaurus had a strong bite and gripped prey animals with its teeth so they could not get away.

- This hunter did not chew its food; it either swallowed prey whole or bit off large chunks.

- Tylosaurus swam in shallow water and attacked all kinds of animals—it even pulled land animals into the water.

Fact file

Found in: Seas of North America

Meaning of name: Knob lizard

Length: 45 feet

Weight: 20,000 pounds

Lived: 85–80 million years ago

Diet: Fish, turtles, and other reptiles

Dimetrodon

- Dimetrodon was a giant hunter that lived long before the dinosaurs.

- It was more closely related to today's mammals than to dinosaurs or other ancient reptiles.

- Dimetrodon had a huge "sail" made of skin and bone spikes on its back.

- Scientists believe that the sail helped Dimetrodon warm up in the sun so that it could run faster than its cold-blooded prey.

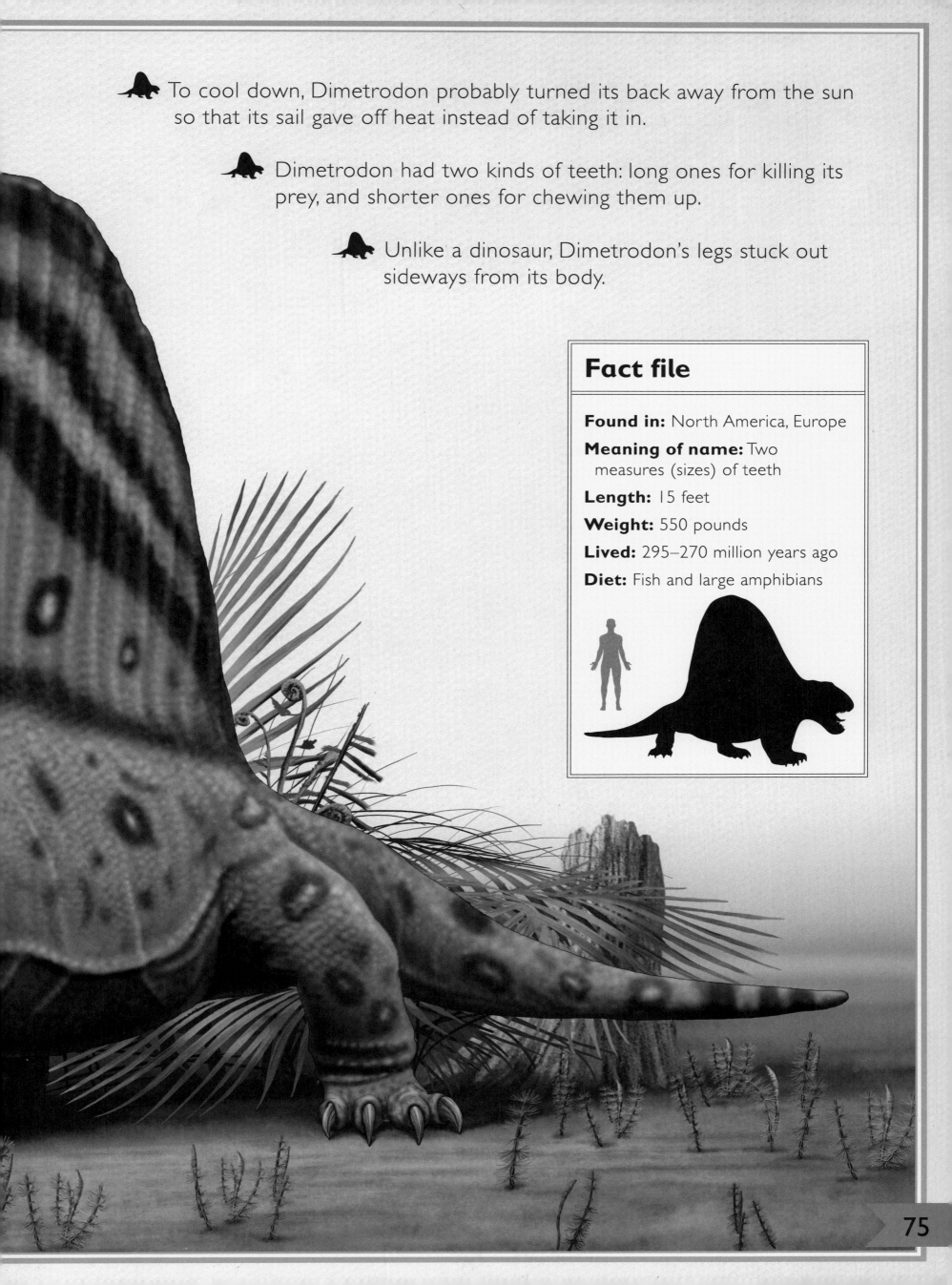

To cool down, Dimetrodon probably turned its back away from the sun so that its sail gave off heat instead of taking it in.

Dimetrodon had two kinds of teeth: long ones for killing its prey, and shorter ones for chewing them up.

Unlike a dinosaur, Dimetrodon's legs stuck out sideways from its body.

Fact file

Found in: North America, Europe

Meaning of name: Two measures (sizes) of teeth

Length: 15 feet

Weight: 550 pounds

Lived: 295–270 million years ago

Diet: Fish and large amphibians

Gastonia

- This armored dinosaur lived in dry forests and chewed on twigs and leaves.

- Its body and tail were covered in spikes and armor plates.

- Sideways-pointing spikes, especially on its tail, were used to fight off predators.

- The upward-pointing spikes on its back may have helped males look bigger in battles for mates with other Gastonia males.

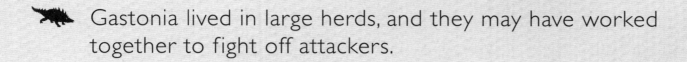 Gastonia lived in large herds, and they may have worked together to fight off attackers.

Evidence suggests that Gastonia males head-butted each other in tests of strength.

This dinosaur had no armor on its belly, but it was very hard for predators to push it over and bite it.

Fact file

Found in: North America

Meaning of name: Gaston's reptile

Length: 15 feet

Weight: 4,000 pounds

Lived: 125 million years ago

Diet: Plants

Sarcosuchus

- Sarcosuchus was the largest crocodile-like reptile that ever lived.

- These creatures were not dinosaurs, but they lived at the same time and were closely related to them.

- Sarcosuchus was twice as big as the largest modern crocodiles.

- Sarcosuchus had a round lump on its snout. Scientists believe this was probably used to make calls in the water.

Fact file

Found in: Africa, South America

Meaning of name: Flesh crocodile

Length: 39 feet

Weight: 18,000 pounds

Lived: 112 million years ago

Diet: Dinosaurs and large fish

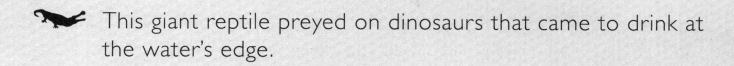 This giant reptile preyed on dinosaurs that came to drink at the water's edge.

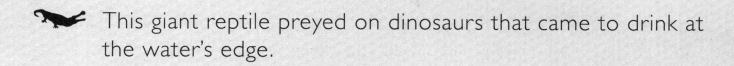 The bite of Sarcosuchus was probably twice as powerful as that of a T. rex.

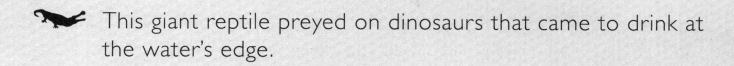 Their eyes looked upward and not forward, so they could watch for prey while hiding under the water.

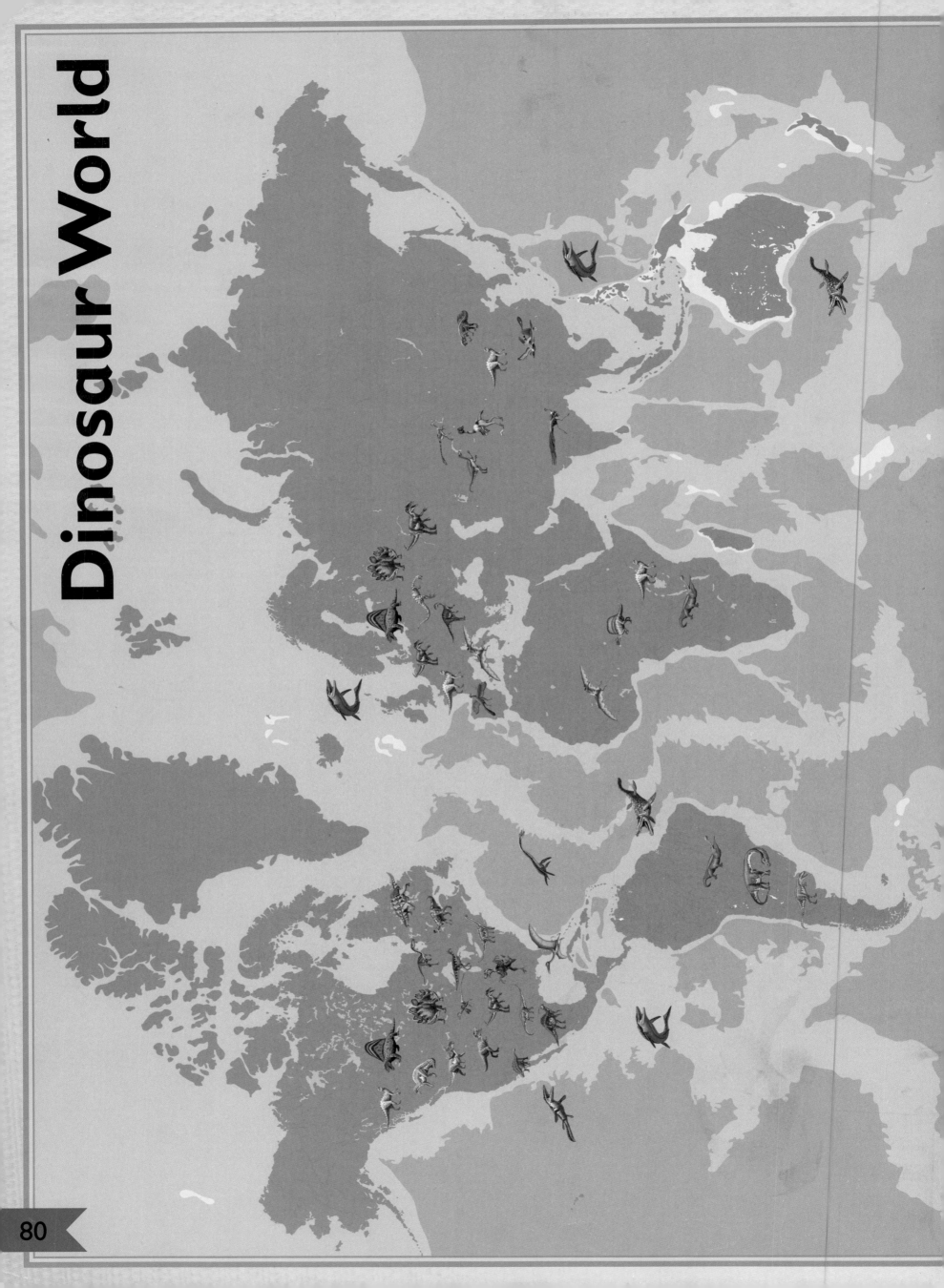